THE INSPIRATION FACTORY
426 HAY STREET, SUBIACO WA 6008
PHONE: (08) 9381 4612
www.inspirationfactory.com.au

AXIOM PUBLISHERS

ISBN 0 947338 52 7

Copyright © Axiom Publishers, 1994
Reprinted, 1995
Reprinted, 1998
Reprinted, 1999

This book is copyright. Apart from any fair dealing for the purpose of private study, research, criticism or review, as permitted under the Copyright act, no part may be reproduced by any process without written permission. Enquiries should be made to the publisher.

Axiom
Australia

This Precious Earth

*Illustrations by
Jan Gallehawk*

This Precious Earth

*A statement about the environment
attributed to Chief Seattle and
presented to the American Congress
in the late 1800's.
Pertinent then — relevant now.
Provocative thoughtful prose to guide
our steps upon this precious earth.*

*The Great Chief in Washington sends word
that he wishes to buy our land.
The great chief also sends us
words of friendship and goodwill,
this is kind of him
since we know he has little need
of our friendship in return.
But we will consider your offer,
we know that if we do not sell,
the white men might come with guns
and take our land.*

How can you buy and sell the sky?
The warmth of the land?
The idea is strange to us.
If we do not own the freshness of the air
and the sparkle of the water
how can you buy them?
Every part of this earth is sacred to my
people.
Every shining pine needle,
every sand shore,
every mist in the dark woods,
every clearing, and humming insect is holy
in the memory and experience of my people.
The sap which courses through the trees
carries the memories.

*The white man's dead
forget the country of their birth
when they go to walk among the stars.
Our dead never forget this beautiful earth,
for it is the mother of the red man,
we are part of the earth,
and it is part of us.*

*The perfumed flowers are our sisters;
the deer, the horse, the great eagle,
these are our brothers.
The rocky crest,
the juices in the meadows,
the body heat of the pony,
and man,
all belong to the same family.
So when the Great Chief in Washington
sends word that he wishes to buy our land,
he asks much of us.*

*The Great Chief sends word
that he will reserve us a place
so that we can live comfortably
to ourselves.
He will be our father
and we will be his children.
So we will consider your offer
to buy our land, but it will not be easy.
For this land is sacred to us.*

*Shining water that moves
in the streams and rivers
is not just water
but the blood of the ancestors.
If we sell,
you must remember that it is sacred
and you must teach your children
that it is sacred,
and that every ghostly reflection
in the clear water of the lakes
tells of events and memories
and the life of my people.*

*The water's murmur is the voice
of my father's father.
The rivers are our brothers,
they quench our thirst.
The rivers carry our canoes
and feed our children.
If we sell you our land
you must remember
and teach your children
that the rivers are our brothers
and yours,
and you must henceforth
give the rivers the kindness
you would give any brother.*

*The red man has always retreated
before advancing white man,
as the mists of the mountain
run before the morning sun.
The ashes of our fathers are sacred,
their graves are holy ground,
and so these hills, these trees,
this portion of the earth
is consecrated to us.*

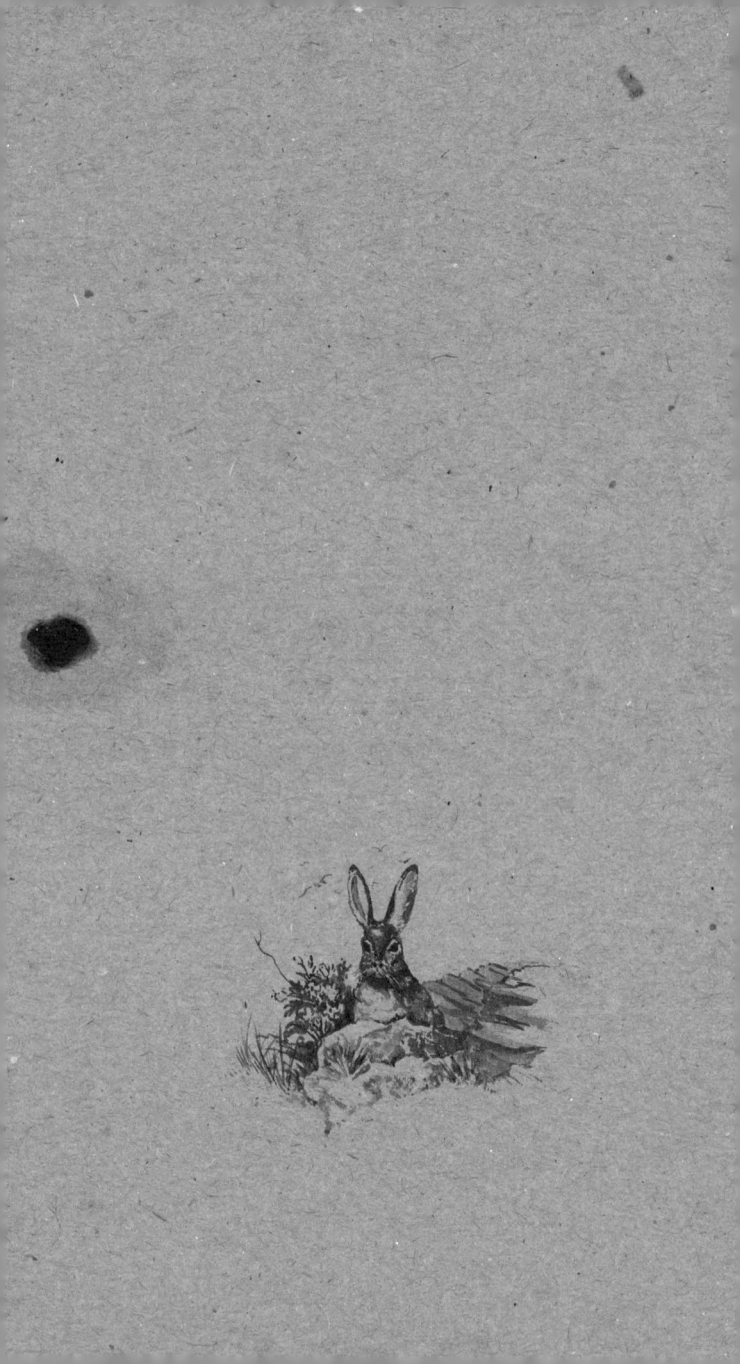

*We know the white man
does not understand our ways,
one portion of land is the same to him
as the next,
but he is a stranger who comes in the night
and takes from the land whatever he needs.
The earth is not his brother,
but his enemy,
and when he has conquered it,
he moves on.
He leaves his fathers' graves and his
childrens' birth rights are forgotten.
He treats his mother the earth,
and his brother the sky,
as things to be bought, plundered,
sold like sheep or beads.*

*His appetite will devour the earth
and leave behind only a desert.
I do not know.
Our ways are different from your ways. The sight of your cities
pains the eyes of the red man
but perhaps it's because the red man
is a savage and does not understand. There's no quiet place
in the white man's cities,
no place to hear the
unfurling of leaves in spring
or the rustle of insects wings.
But perhaps it's because I am a savage
and do not understand.*

*The clatter seems only to insult the ears,
and what is there to life
if a man can not hear a lonely cry
of the whip-poor-will
or the arguments of a frog
around the pool at night?*

*I am a red man and do not understand,
the Indian prefers the soft sound of wind
darting over the face of the pond,
and the smell of the wind itself,
cleansed by the midday rain,
or scented with the pine.*

*The air is precious to the red man,
for all things share the same breath,
the beast, the tree, the man,
they all share the same breath.
The white man doesn't seem to notice
the air he breathes,
like a man dying for many days,
he his numb to the stench.*

*If we sell you our land
you must remember
that the air is precious to us,
that the air shares its spirit
with all the life it supports.
The wind that gave our grandfather
his first breath
also receives his last sigh,
and the wind must also give our children
the spirit of life.*

*And if we sell you our land
you must keep it apart and sacred,
as a place where even the white man
can go to taste the wind
that is sweetened
by the meadow's flowers.*

*So we will consider your offer
to buy our land,
and if we decide to accept,
I will make one condition;
the white man must treat the beasts
of this land as his brothers.
I am a savage
and do not understand any other way.
I have seen a thousand rotting buffaloes
on the prairie,
left by the white man
who shot them from a passing train.*

*I am a savage and do not understand
how the smoking iron horse
can be more important
than the buffalo we kill only to stay alive.*

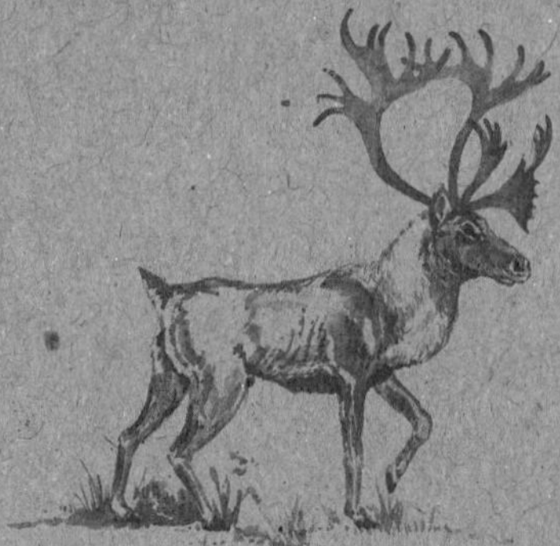

*What is man without the beasts?
If all the beasts were gone,
men would die
from the great loneliness of spirit;
for whatever happens to the beasts
soon happens to man.
All things are connected.*

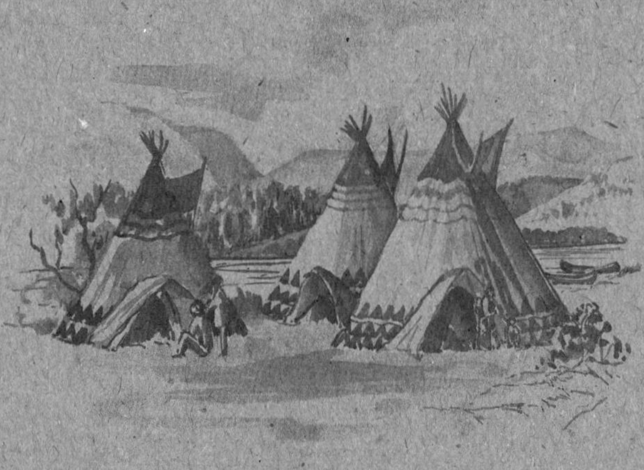

*You must teach your children
that the ground beneath their feet
is the ashes of our grandfathers,
so they will respect the land.
Tell your children
that the earth is rich
with the lives of our kin.
Teach your children
what we taught our children.
That the earth is our mother.*

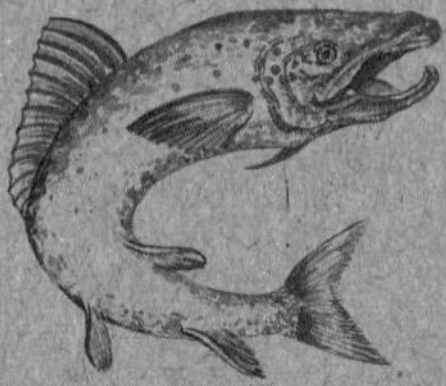

*Whatever befalls the earth,
befalls the sons of the earth.
If men spit upon the ground,
they spit upon themselves.
This we know,
the earth doesn't belong to man;
man belongs to the earth.
This we know,
all things are connected,
like the blood that unites one family.*

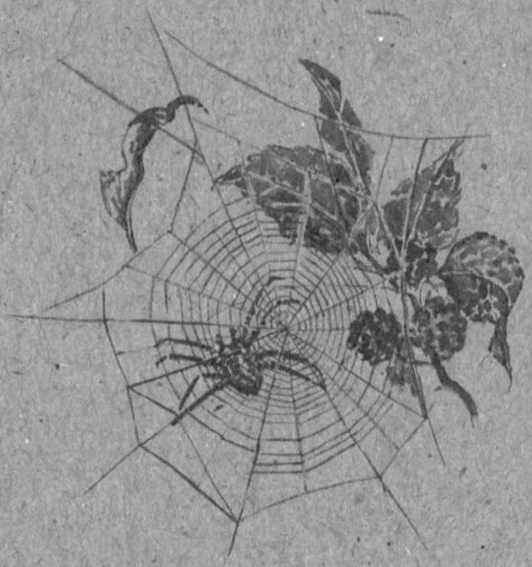

*All things are connected,
whatever befalls the earth,
befalls the sons of the earth.
Man didn't weave the web of life;
he is merely a strand in it.
Whatever he does to the web,
he does to himself.*

*But, we will consider your offer
to go to the reservation
you have for my people.
We will live apart in peace.
It matters little where we pass
the rest of our days.
There are not many.
A few more hours, a few more winters,
and none of the children
of the great tribes
that once lived on this earth,
or that roam now in small bands
in the woods,
will be left to mourn
the graves of people
once as powerful and hopeful as yours.*

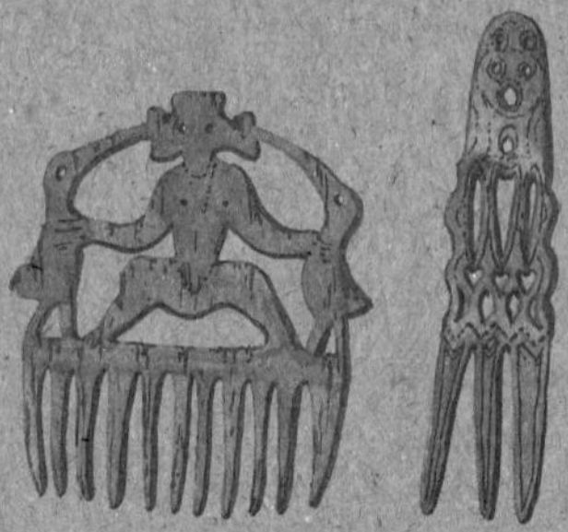

*But why should I mourn
the passing of my people.
Tribes are made of men,
nothing more.
Men come and go
like the waves of the sea.*

*Even the white man
whose God walks and talks to him
as friend to friend,
cannot be exempted
from the common destiny.
We may be brothers after all.
We shall see.*

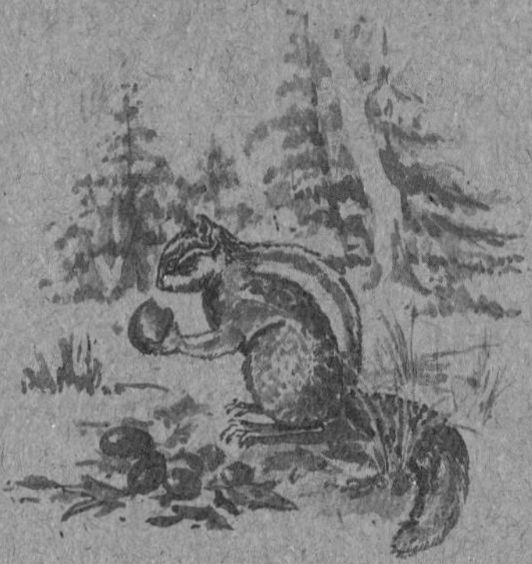

*One thing we know which the white man
may one day discover,
our God is the same God.
You may think now that you own Him,
as you wish to own our land;
but you cannot.
He is the God of man,
and His compassion is equal
to the red man and the white.*

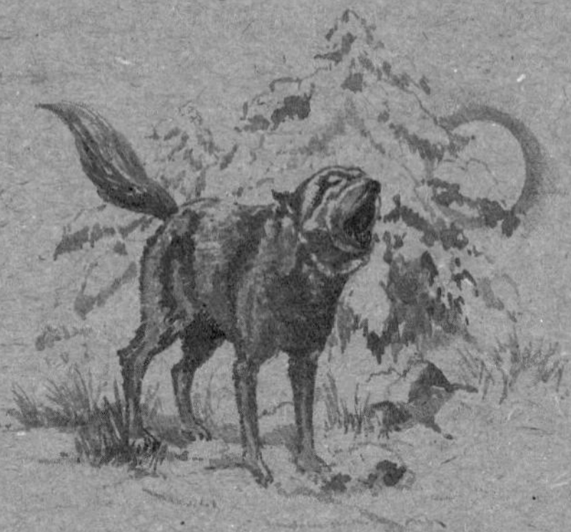

*This earth is precious to Him,
to harm the earth
is to heap contempt on it's Creator.
The whites too shall pass;
perhaps sooner than all other tribes.
Continue to contaminate your bed,
and one day you'll suffocate
in your own waste.
But in your perishing
you will shine brightly,
fired by the strength of the God
who brought you to this land,
and for some special purpose
gave you dominion over this land
and over the red man.*

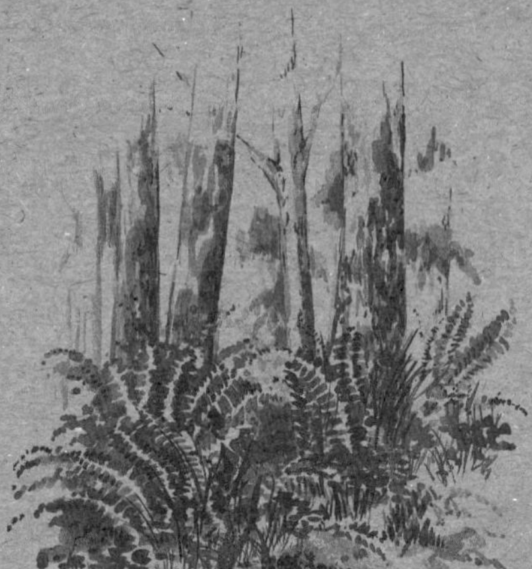

*That destiny is a mystery to us.
For we do not understand
when the buffalo are all slaughtered,
the wild horses tamed,
the secret corners of the forest
heavy with the scent of many men,
the view of the ripe fields
blotted by talking wires.*

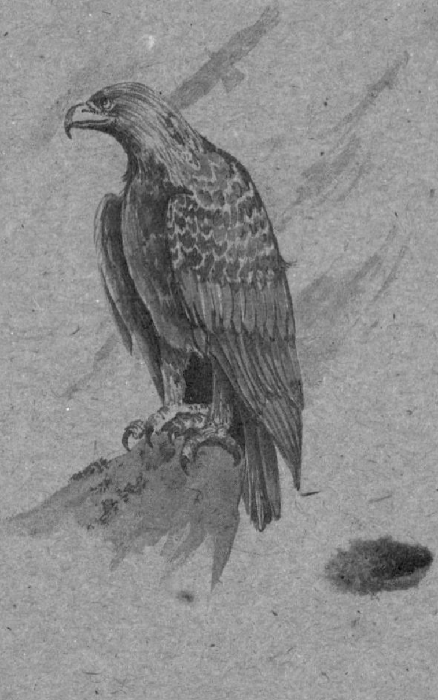

*Where is the thicket?
Gone.
Where is the eagle?
Gone.
And what is it to say goodbye
to the swift pony and the hunt?
The end of living
and beginning of survival.*

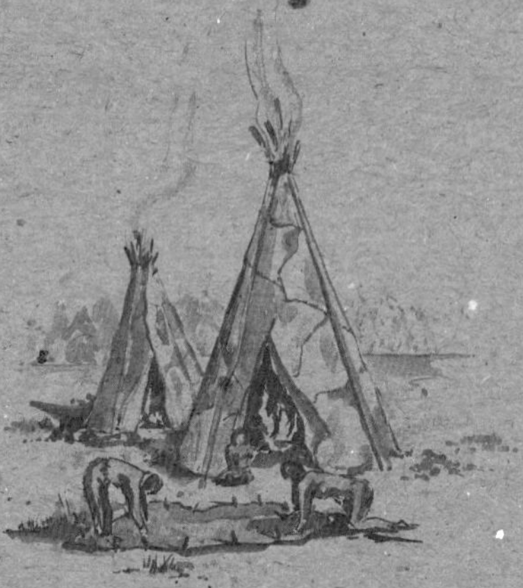

*So we will consider your offer
to buy our land.
If we agree,
it will be to secure the reservation
you have promised;
then perhaps we may live out
our brief days as we wish.
When the last red man
has vanished from the earth,
and his memory is only a shadow
of a cloud moving across the prairie,
these shores and forest
will still hold the spirits of my people,
for they love this earth
as the new born
loves it's mother's heart-beat.*

*So if we sell you our land,
love it as we have loved it,
care for it as we have cared for it.
Hold in your mind
the memory of the land
as it is when you take it.*

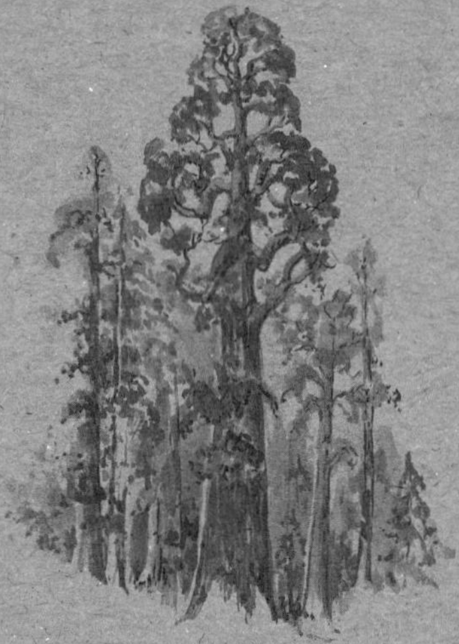

*With all your strength,
with all your mind,
with all your heart,
preserve it for your children,
and love it
as God loves us all.*

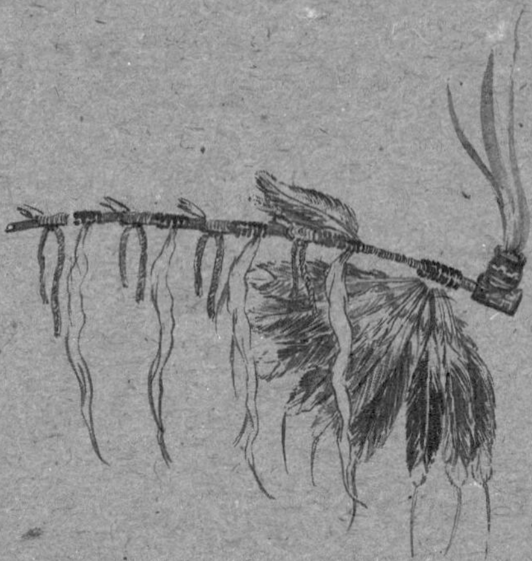

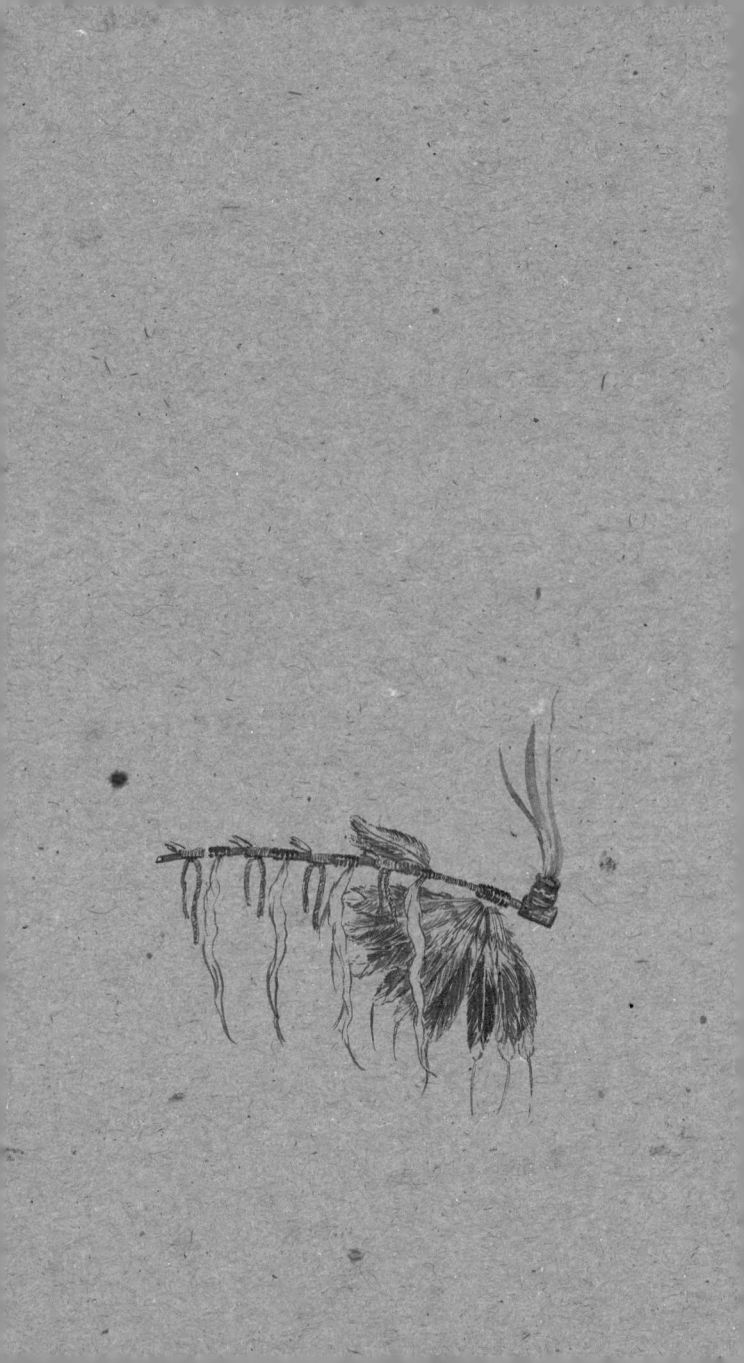

*One thing we know
our God is the same God.*

*This earth is precious to Him.
Even the white man cannot be exempt
from the common destiny.*

*We may be brothers after all.
We shall see!*